History Of Zimbabwe For Kids

A History Series

Children Explore Histories Of The World Edition

Speedy Publishing LLC
40 E. Main St. #1156
Newark, DE 19711
www.speedypublishing.com

The name "Zimbabwe" is derived from two words of Shona language 'dzimba' ('houses') and 'mabwe' ('stones') and can be translated into English as 'Big houses of stones' or 'honorable houses'.

L. Kariba
Maramba
Binga
ZIMI
Bulawa
Maun
BOTSWANA

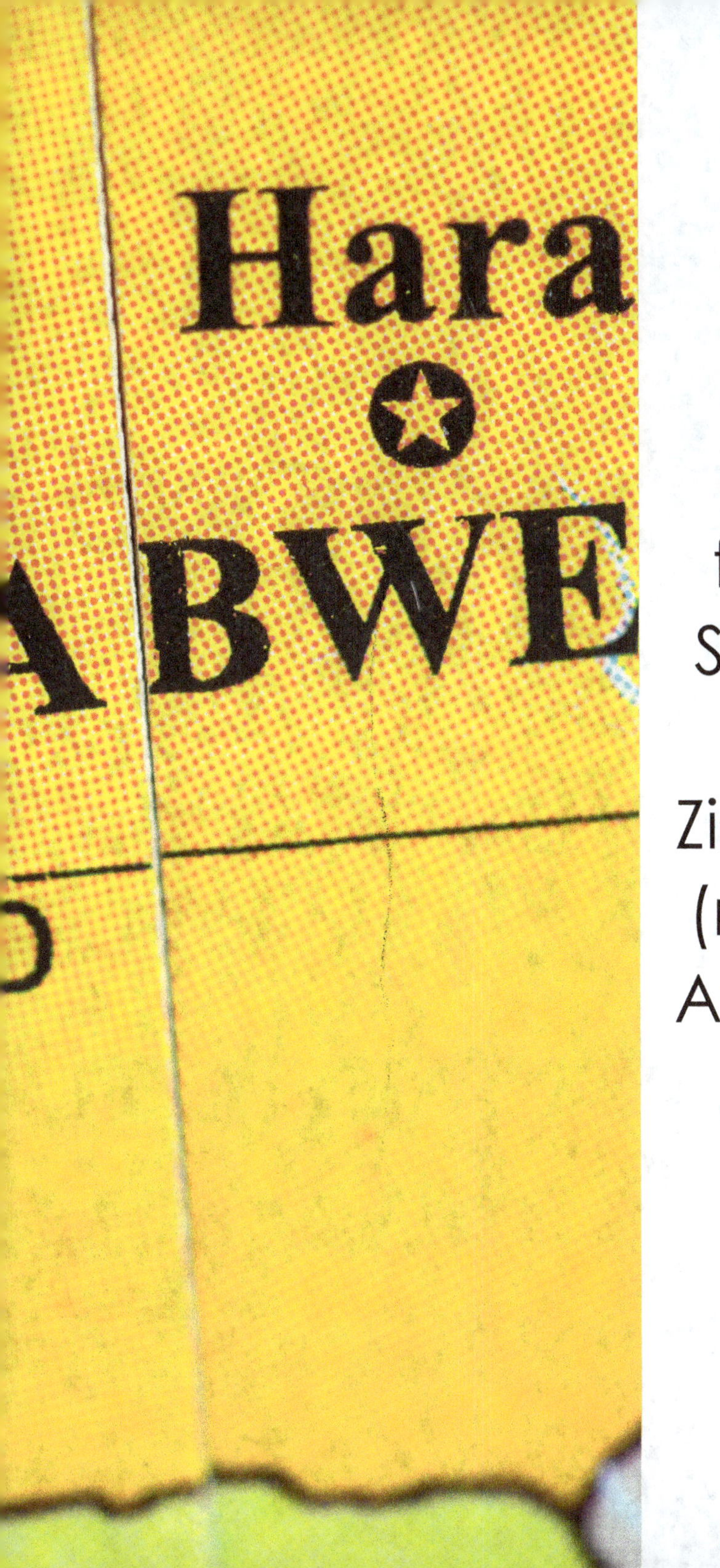

Zimbabwe was formerly known as Southern Rhodesia, Rhodesia and Zimbabwe Rhodesia (named after South African businessman Cecil Rhodes).

In 1000 AD, Shona people began their rule and built a city called Zimbabwe.

In 1400s,
Karanga branch
of the Shona
established the
Mwanamutapa
Empire.

By 1500,
Christianity was
introduced by
the Portuguese
explorers.

Lobengula, the ruler, signed an agreement that granted mineral rights to the British South African Company in 1888.

ZAMBIA
Kariba
Lake Kariba
Livingstone
Victoria Falls
Hwange
Chitung
ZIMBAB
Kw
Bulawayo
Zvish
Gwanda
BOTSWANA
Rio
Musina

The British South African Company occupied the region and called the territory Rhodesia by 1893.

UNIVERSAL POST
1874
1919
NORTHERN
RHODESIA

Great Britain recognized southern and northern Rhodesia as separate territories.

Southern Rhodesia became a self-governing British Colony by 1923.

In 1953, Great Britain set up the Federation of Rhodesia and Nyasaland, which included the territories of Southern and Northern Rhodesia.

It was 1963 when the Federation of Rhodesia and Nyasaland was dissolved.

A year after, Northern Rhodesia became Zambia and Southern Rhodesia became known as Rhodesia.

November 11, 1965, Prime Minister, Ian Smith, declared Rhodesia independent. Great Britain declared this action illegal and banned trade with Rhodesia.

Then the United Nations imposed sanctions on Rhodesia in 1966.

In 1969, a new
constitution was
introduced to
prevent black
Africans from
ever gaining
control of the
government.

In 1970-1974, the Civil War between government troops and black guerrillas began.

From 1977-1979 Prime Minister Smith began to make plans to establish a new government with a majority of black leaders.

It was by April 18, 1980, when Great Britain recognized the country's independence and Rhodesia's name was officially changed to Zimbabwe.

The **History of Zimbabwe** is very rich, research and learn more!

Visit

BABY PROFESSOR
EDUCATION KIDS

www.BabyProfessorBooks.com

to download Free Baby Professor eBooks
and view our catalog of new and exciting
Children's Books